We Work at the Vet's

Angela Aylmore

Little Nippers

H www.heinemann.co.uk/library
Visit our website to find out more information about **Heinemann Library** books.

To order:
☎ Phone 44 (0) 1865 888066
▤ Send a fax to 44 (0) 1865 314091
▣ Visit the Heinemann Bookshop at www.heinemann.co.uk/library to browse our catalogue and order online.

First published in Great Britain by Heinemann Library, Halley Court, Jordan Hill, Oxford OX2 8EJ, part of Harcourt Education.
Heinemann is a registered trademark of Harcourt Education Ltd.

Editorial: Isabel Thomas and Sarah Chappelow
Design: Jo Hinton-Malivoire and bigtop
Picture Research: Erica Newbery
Production: Duncan Gilbert

Originated by RMW
Printed and bound in China by South China Printing Company

ISBN: 978 0 431 16491 5 (hardback)
10 09 08 07
10 9 8 7 6 5 4 3 2 1

ISBN: 978 0 431 16496 0 (paperback)
11 10 09 08 07
10 9 8 7 6 5 4 3 2 1

British Library Cataloguing in Publication Data
Aylmore, Angela
We work at the vet's. - (Where we work)
636'.089
A full catalogue record for this book is available from the British Library.

Acknowledgements
The publishers would like to thank the following for permission to reproduce photographs:
Alamy p. **15** (Network Photographers Ltd); Ardea pp. **4–5** (John Daniels), **19** (John Daniels); Corbis p. **6–7** (Royalty Free), **8** (Tom Stewart); Getty Images p. **14** (Photodisc); Holt Studios p. **16**; Naturepl.com p. **9** (T J Rich); Photolibary pp. **10–11** (Creatas); Rex Features pp. **12–13**, **21**.

Quiz pp. **22–23**: **astronaut** (Getty/Photodisc), **brush and comb** (Corbis/DK Limited), **doctor** (Getty Images/Photodisc), **firefighter helmet** (Corbis), **ladder** (Corbis/Royalty Free), **scrubs** (Corbis), **space food** (Alamy/Hugh Threlfall), **stethoscope** (Getty Images/Photodisc), **thermometer** (Getty Images/Photodisc).

Cover photograph of a vet reproduced with permission of Corbis.

Every effort has been made to contact copyright holders of any material reproduced in this book. Any omissions will be rectified in subsequent printings if notice is given to the publishers.

The paper used to print this book comes from sustainable resources.

Some words are shown in bold, **like this**. They are explained in the glossary on page 24.

Contents

Welcome to the vet's!

This is a vet's **surgery**.

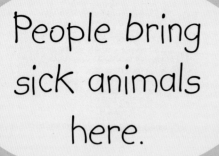

People bring sick animals here.

Working as a vet

I am a vet.

Vets help sick animals
to get better again.

What I wear

In the **surgery** I wear a white coat.

When I visit a farm I wear normal clothes and strong boots.

An operation

I wear gloves and special clothes for an **operation**.

They stop **germs** from getting on the animals.

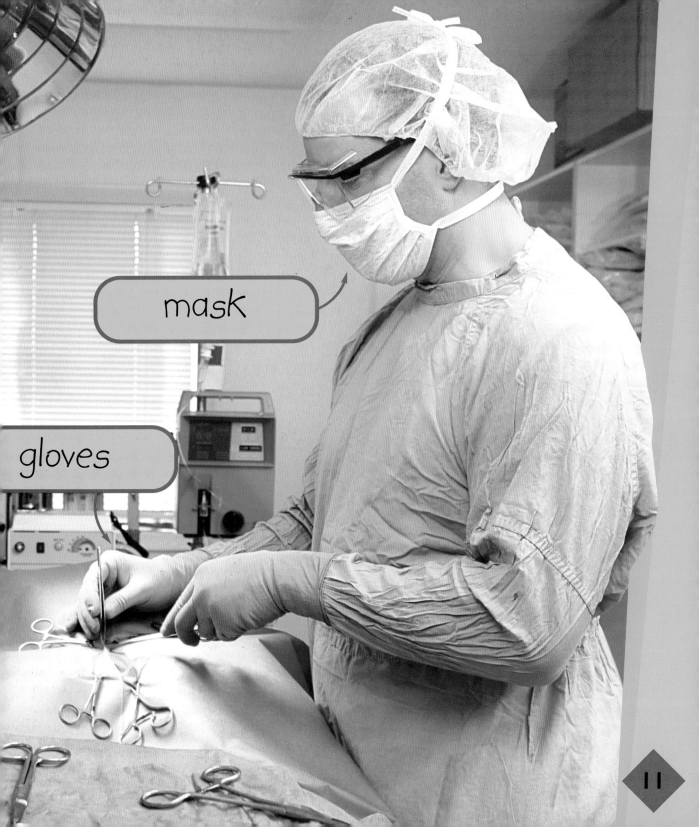

mask

gloves

11

A collar

This cat has had an **operation**.

The collar stops the cat licking the **stitches**.

Heartbeats

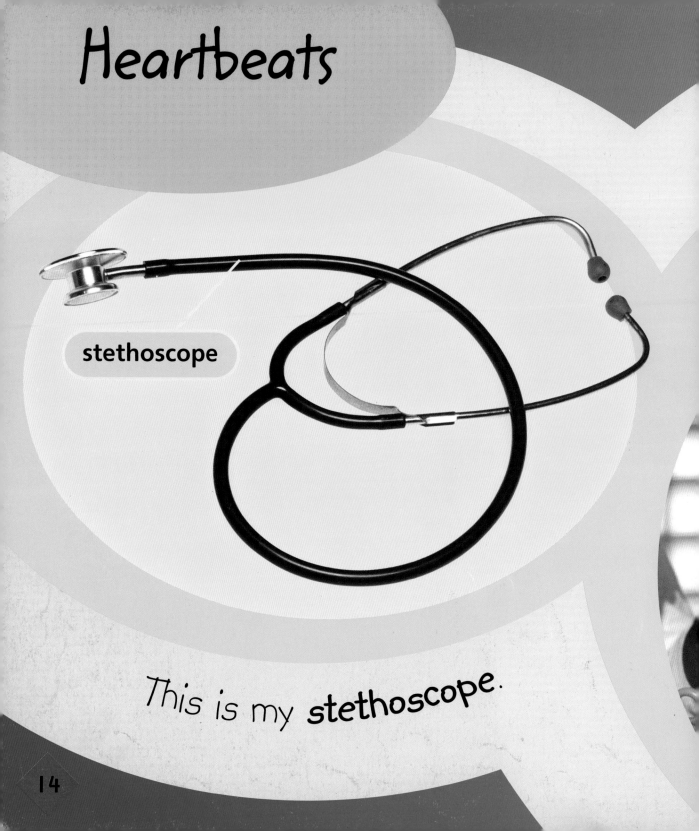

stethoscope

This is my stethoscope.

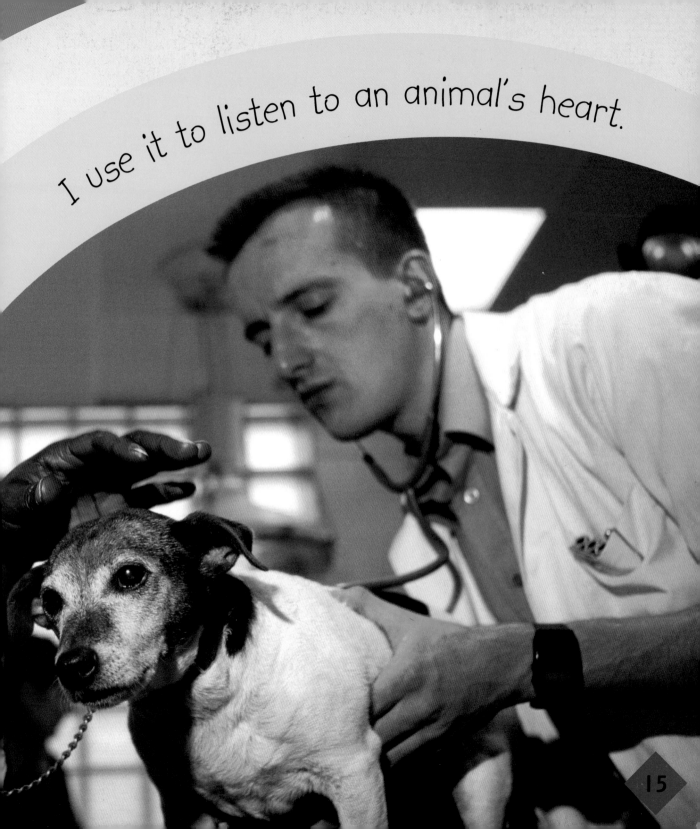

I use it to listen to an animal's heart.

15

Clip, clip!

This rabbit's claws are too long.

clippers

I use special **clippers** to cut them.

Visiting a farm

Sometimes I visit
animals on the farm.

I give them medicine to make them better.

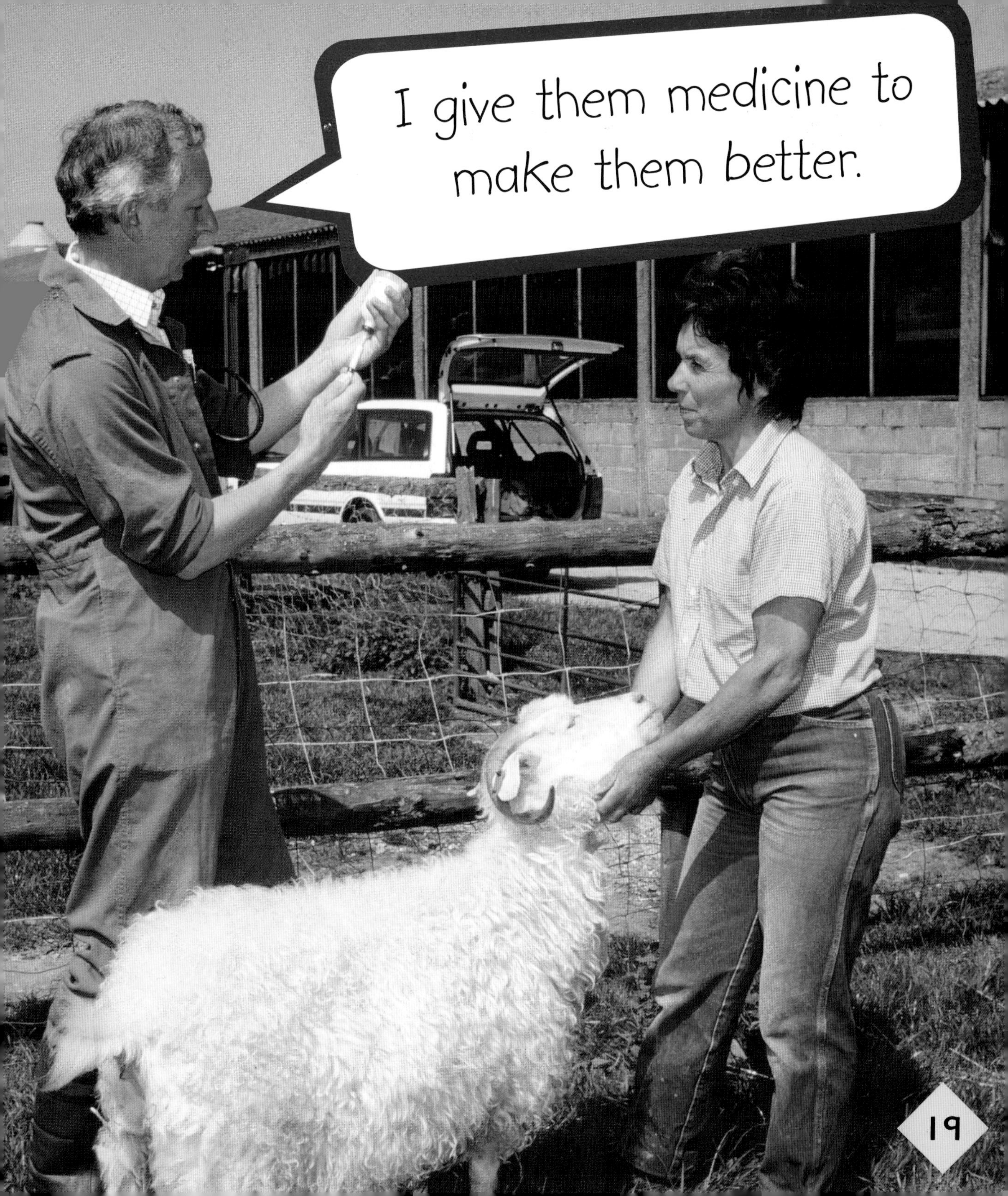

Night time

Some animals have to stay at the vet's over night.

A nurse looks after the animals until the morning.

Quiz

space food

Do you want to be a vet? Which of these things would you need?

stethoscope

spacesuit

helmet

ladder

combs and brushes

nurse's uniform

thermometer

white coat

23

Glossary

clippers special tool for cutting animals' claws

germs things in the air that can make you ill

operation a way of making an animal better

stethoscope what a vet uses to listen to an animal's heartbeat

stitches thread used to sew up a cut

surgery place where the vet looks after sick animals

Index

Notes for adults

This series supports the young child's exploration of their learning environment and their knowledge and understanding of their world. The following Early Learning Goals are relevant to the series:

- Respond to significant experiences, showing a range of feelings where appropriate.
- Find out about events they observe.
- Ask questions about why things happen and how things work.
- Find out and identify the uses of everyday technology to support their learning.

The series shows the different jobs professionals do in four different environments. There are opportunities to compare and contrast the jobs and provide an understanding of what each entails.

The books will help the child to extend their vocabulary, as they will hear new words. Some of the words that may be new to them in **We Work at the Vet's** are *surgery*, *operation*, *germs*, *stitches*, *clippers*, and *stethoscope*. Since the words are used in context in the book this should enable the young child to gradually incorporate them into their own vocabulary.

Follow-up activities
The child could role play situations in a vet's surgery. Areas could be set up to create a consulting room, operating theatre, and cages for in-patients. The child could also record what they have found out by drawing, painting, or tape recording their experiences.

24